50 Everyday Chef Recipes

By: Kelly Johnson

Table of Contents

- Spaghetti Aglio e Olio
- Chicken Stir Fry with Vegetables
- Veggie Tacos with Avocado
- Lemon Garlic Salmon
- One-Pan Baked Chicken and Veggies
- Beef and Broccoli Stir Fry
- Margherita Pizza
- Chicken Caesar Salad
- Garlic Butter Shrimp Pasta
- Roasted Sweet Potato and Black Bean Bowls
- Caprese Salad
- BBQ Chicken Quesadillas
- Spinach and Ricotta Stuffed Chicken
- Baked Ziti with Marinara
- Grilled Cheese with Tomato Soup
- Sweet and Sour Chicken
- Veggie Fried Rice

- Chicken Fajitas
- Teriyaki Chicken Skewers
- Pesto Pasta with Cherry Tomatoes
- Tofu Stir Fry with Peanut Sauce
- Lemon Herb Grilled Chicken
- Avocado Toast with Egg
- Garlic Parmesan Roasted Potatoes
- Spicy Tuna Poke Bowl
- Shrimp Tacos with Lime Crema
- Chickpea Salad Sandwich
- Beef Tacos with Salsa Verde
- Chicken Parmesan
- Stuffed Bell Peppers
- Shrimp Scampi
- Mushroom Risotto
- Tomato Basil Soup with Grilled Cheese Croutons
- Chicken and Rice Casserole
- Baked Chicken Fajita Bowl
- Roasted Vegetable Soup

- Avocado and Egg Breakfast Burrito

- Pappardelle with Creamy Mushroom Sauce

- Chicken Pot Pie

- Spaghetti Carbonara

- Roasted Garlic and Parmesan Brussels Sprouts

- Veggie and Hummus Wrap

- Sloppy Joes

- Lemon Basil Pesto Chicken

- Sausage and Peppers

- Grilled Veggie Skewers with Quinoa

- Baked Salmon with Asparagus

- Stuffed Portobello Mushrooms

- Sweet Potato and Chickpea Curry

- Chicken Shawarma Bowls

Spaghetti Aglio e Olio

Ingredients:

- 8 oz spaghetti
- 4 garlic cloves, thinly sliced
- 1/4 tsp red pepper flakes
- 1/4 cup olive oil
- Fresh parsley, chopped
- Salt, to taste
- Grated Parmesan (optional)

Instructions:

1. Cook spaghetti according to package instructions.
2. While pasta cooks, sauté garlic and red pepper flakes in olive oil over low heat until fragrant.
3. Toss the cooked pasta in the garlic oil, season with salt, and top with fresh parsley.
4. Optionally, sprinkle with Parmesan before serving.

Chicken Stir Fry with Vegetables

Ingredients:

- 2 chicken breasts, thinly sliced
- 1 cup bell peppers, sliced
- 1/2 cup carrots, julienned
- 1/2 cup broccoli florets
- 2 tbsp soy sauce
- 1 tbsp hoisin sauce
- 1 tbsp sesame oil
- 2 garlic cloves, minced
- 1 tbsp ginger, grated

Instructions:

1. Heat sesame oil in a pan, cook chicken until browned. Remove and set aside.
2. In the same pan, sauté garlic and ginger. Add veggies and cook until tender.
3. Return chicken to the pan, add soy sauce and hoisin sauce, and stir-fry until well combined.

Veggie Tacos with Avocado

Ingredients:

- 1 cup black beans, cooked
- 1 cup corn kernels
- 1 avocado, sliced
- 1/2 cup red onion, sliced
- 1/2 cup cilantro, chopped
- 8 small tortillas
- Lime wedges
- Optional: salsa, sour cream, cheese

Instructions:

1. Warm tortillas and fill with beans, corn, avocado, onion, and cilantro.
2. Top with salsa or sour cream if desired. Serve with lime wedges.

Lemon Garlic Salmon

Ingredients:

- 2 salmon fillets
- 2 tbsp olive oil
- 3 garlic cloves, minced
- Juice of 1 lemon
- Salt and pepper, to taste
- Fresh parsley for garnish

Instructions:

1. Preheat oven to 400°F (200°C).
2. In a small bowl, mix olive oil, garlic, lemon juice, salt, and pepper.
3. Place salmon fillets on a baking sheet, drizzle with the lemon garlic mixture.
4. Bake for 12-15 minutes, until salmon is cooked through. Garnish with parsley.

One-Pan Baked Chicken and Veggies

Ingredients:

- 2 chicken breasts
- 1 cup baby potatoes, halved
- 1 cup carrots, chopped
- 1 tbsp olive oil
- 1 tsp paprika
- 1 tsp garlic powder
- Salt and pepper, to taste

Instructions:

1. Preheat oven to 400°F (200°C).
2. Toss chicken and veggies in olive oil, paprika, garlic powder, salt, and pepper.
3. Place on a baking sheet and bake for 25-30 minutes, until chicken is cooked and veggies are tender.

Beef and Broccoli Stir Fry

Ingredients:

- 1 lb beef (flank steak or sirloin), thinly sliced
- 2 cups broccoli florets
- 1 tbsp soy sauce
- 2 tbsp oyster sauce
- 1 tbsp sesame oil
- 2 garlic cloves, minced
- 1 tsp ginger, grated

Instructions:

1. Heat sesame oil in a pan, sauté beef until browned. Remove and set aside.
2. In the same pan, cook garlic and ginger, then add broccoli and cook for 3-4 minutes.
3. Return beef to the pan, add soy sauce and oyster sauce, and stir-fry for another 2 minutes.

Margherita Pizza

Ingredients:

- 1 pizza dough (store-bought or homemade)
- 1/2 cup tomato sauce
- 8 oz fresh mozzarella, sliced
- Fresh basil leaves
- Olive oil for drizzling

Instructions:

1. Preheat oven to 475°F (245°C).
2. Roll out the pizza dough and spread tomato sauce evenly.
3. Top with mozzarella and bake for 10-12 minutes, until crust is golden.
4. Remove from oven, add fresh basil, and drizzle with olive oil.

Chicken Caesar Salad

Ingredients:

- 2 chicken breasts, grilled and sliced
- 4 cups Romaine lettuce, chopped
- 1/2 cup Caesar dressing
- Croutons
- Freshly grated Parmesan

Instructions:

1. Toss lettuce with Caesar dressing in a large bowl.
2. Add sliced grilled chicken and toss again.
3. Top with croutons and Parmesan before serving.

Garlic Butter Shrimp Pasta

Ingredients:

- 8 oz spaghetti or your preferred pasta
- 1 lb shrimp, peeled and deveined
- 4 tbsp butter
- 4 garlic cloves, minced
- 1/2 cup chicken broth
- 1/2 cup heavy cream
- Fresh parsley, chopped
- Grated Parmesan, for topping

Instructions:

1. Cook pasta according to package instructions.
2. In a skillet, melt butter and sauté garlic until fragrant.
3. Add shrimp and cook until pink, then pour in chicken broth and cream.
4. Toss in cooked pasta, season with salt and pepper, and top with parsley and Parmesan.

Roasted Sweet Potato and Black Bean Bowls

Ingredients:

- 2 medium sweet potatoes, peeled and cubed
- 1 can black beans, drained and rinsed
- 1 tbsp olive oil
- 1 tsp cumin
- 1/2 tsp chili powder
- Salt and pepper to taste
- 1/4 cup cilantro, chopped
- Lime wedges for serving
- Optional toppings: avocado, salsa, sour cream

Instructions:

1. Preheat oven to 400°F (200°C).
2. Toss sweet potato cubes in olive oil, cumin, chili powder, salt, and pepper.
3. Roast for 25-30 minutes, until tender.
4. In bowls, layer roasted sweet potatoes, black beans, and cilantro. Serve with lime wedges and optional toppings.

Caprese Salad

Ingredients:

- 2 large tomatoes, sliced
- 8 oz fresh mozzarella, sliced
- Fresh basil leaves
- 2 tbsp olive oil
- 1 tbsp balsamic vinegar
- Salt and pepper to taste

Instructions:

1. Arrange tomato slices, mozzarella, and basil on a plate.
2. Drizzle with olive oil and balsamic vinegar.
3. Sprinkle with salt and pepper before serving.

BBQ Chicken Quesadillas

Ingredients:

- 2 cups cooked chicken, shredded
- 1/2 cup BBQ sauce
- 1 cup shredded cheese (cheddar or mozzarella)
- 4 flour tortillas
- 1 tbsp olive oil

Instructions:

1. Toss shredded chicken with BBQ sauce.
2. Heat a pan with a little olive oil. Place one tortilla in the pan, sprinkle with cheese, top with BBQ chicken, and cover with another tortilla.
3. Cook until golden brown, then flip and cook the other side.
4. Slice and serve with sour cream or guacamole.

Spinach and Ricotta Stuffed Chicken

Ingredients:

- 4 boneless, skinless chicken breasts
- 1 cup ricotta cheese
- 2 cups spinach, sautéed and drained
- 1/2 cup Parmesan cheese, grated
- 1 tsp garlic powder
- Salt and pepper to taste
- 1 tbsp olive oil

Instructions:

1. Preheat oven to 375°F (190°C).
2. Mix ricotta, spinach, Parmesan, garlic powder, salt, and pepper.
3. Cut a pocket in each chicken breast and stuff with the ricotta mixture.
4. Heat olive oil in a pan, sear the chicken for 2-3 minutes on each side.
5. Transfer to the oven and bake for 20–25 minutes until chicken is cooked through.

Baked Ziti with Marinara

Ingredients:

- 12 oz ziti pasta
- 2 cups marinara sauce
- 1 cup ricotta cheese
- 2 cups shredded mozzarella cheese
- 1/4 cup Parmesan cheese
- 1 tsp dried oregano
- Fresh basil for garnish

Instructions:

1. Preheat oven to 375°F (190°C).
2. Cook pasta according to package instructions. Drain and mix with marinara sauce, ricotta, and oregano.
3. Transfer to a baking dish, top with mozzarella and Parmesan.
4. Bake for 25-30 minutes until cheese is melted and bubbly. Garnish with basil.

Grilled Cheese with Tomato Soup

Ingredients for Grilled Cheese:

- 4 slices bread
- 4 tbsp butter
- 4 slices cheddar cheese

Ingredients for Tomato Soup:

- 1 can tomato soup
- 1/2 cup heavy cream
- 1 tbsp butter
- Salt and pepper to taste

Instructions:

1. For grilled cheese, butter the outside of bread slices, place cheese between slices, and grill on medium heat until golden brown on both sides.
2. For soup, heat tomato soup with butter and heavy cream, simmer for 5 minutes, and season with salt and pepper.
3. Serve grilled cheese with a side of tomato soup.

Sweet and Sour Chicken

Ingredients:

- 2 chicken breasts, diced
- 1/2 cup bell peppers, diced
- 1/2 cup pineapple chunks
- 1/4 cup vinegar
- 1/4 cup sugar
- 1/4 cup ketchup
- 1 tbsp soy sauce
- 1 tbsp cornstarch (optional for thickening)

Instructions:

1. Cook diced chicken in a pan until browned.
2. In a separate bowl, mix vinegar, sugar, ketchup, soy sauce, and cornstarch if using.
3. Add bell peppers, pineapple, and sauce to the chicken. Simmer for 10 minutes until the sauce thickens.
4. Serve over rice.

Veggie Fried Rice

Ingredients:

- 2 cups cooked rice (preferably cold)
- 1 cup mixed vegetables (carrots, peas, corn)
- 2 eggs, scrambled
- 2 tbsp soy sauce
- 1 tbsp sesame oil
- 1/2 tsp garlic powder
- Green onions for garnish

Instructions:

1. Heat sesame oil in a pan, add mixed veggies and cook until tender.
2. Push veggies to one side and scramble eggs in the same pan.
3. Add rice, soy sauce, garlic powder, and stir-fry for 3–5 minutes.
4. Garnish with green onions before serving.

Chicken Fajitas

Ingredients:

- 2 chicken breasts, thinly sliced
- 1 onion, sliced
- 1 bell pepper, sliced
- 1 tbsp olive oil
- 1 tbsp fajita seasoning
- Flour tortillas
- Lime wedges, cilantro, and salsa for serving

Instructions:

1. Heat olive oil in a pan and cook chicken with fajita seasoning.
2. Add onions and bell peppers, cook until tender.
3. Serve in warm tortillas with lime, cilantro, and salsa.

Teriyaki Chicken Skewers

Ingredients:

- 2 chicken breasts, cut into chunks
- 1/4 cup soy sauce
- 2 tbsp honey
- 1 tbsp rice vinegar
- 1 garlic clove, minced
- 1 tsp grated ginger
- 1 tbsp sesame oil
- Skewers (wooden or metal)

Instructions:

1. In a bowl, whisk together soy sauce, honey, rice vinegar, garlic, ginger, and sesame oil to make the marinade.
2. Thread chicken onto skewers and coat with the marinade.
3. Marinate in the fridge for 30 minutes.
4. Preheat grill or broiler to medium-high heat.
5. Grill chicken skewers for 5-7 minutes per side until cooked through. Serve with extra marinade if desired.

Pesto Pasta with Cherry Tomatoes

Ingredients:

- 8 oz pasta (spaghetti, penne, etc.)
- 1/2 cup pesto sauce (store-bought or homemade)
- 1 cup cherry tomatoes, halved
- 1/4 cup Parmesan cheese, grated
- Fresh basil for garnish

Instructions:

1. Cook pasta according to package instructions. Drain and set aside.
2. In a pan, sauté cherry tomatoes until just softened.
3. Toss the cooked pasta with pesto sauce and sautéed tomatoes.
4. Top with grated Parmesan and fresh basil.

Tofu Stir Fry with Peanut Sauce

Ingredients:

- 1 block firm tofu, pressed and cubed
- 1 cup mixed vegetables (carrots, bell peppers, broccoli, etc.)
- 2 tbsp soy sauce
- 1 tbsp sesame oil
- 1/4 cup peanut butter
- 2 tbsp soy sauce
- 1 tbsp honey
- 1 tbsp rice vinegar
- 1 garlic clove, minced
- 1/2 tsp chili flakes (optional)

Instructions:

1. In a pan, sauté tofu cubes in sesame oil until crispy and golden brown. Remove from the pan and set aside.
2. In the same pan, cook mixed vegetables until tender.
3. For the sauce, whisk together peanut butter, soy sauce, honey, rice vinegar, garlic, and chili flakes.
4. Add tofu back into the pan, pour over the peanut sauce, and toss to combine. Serve warm.

Lemon Herb Grilled Chicken

Ingredients:

- 4 chicken breasts
- 2 tbsp olive oil
- Juice and zest of 1 lemon
- 2 garlic cloves, minced
- 1 tsp dried oregano
- Salt and pepper to taste

Instructions:

1. In a bowl, mix olive oil, lemon juice, lemon zest, garlic, oregano, salt, and pepper.
2. Coat the chicken breasts with the marinade and let sit for 30 minutes.
3. Preheat grill to medium heat. Grill chicken for 6-7 minutes per side until fully cooked.
4. Serve with a side of veggies or over a salad.

Avocado Toast with Egg

Ingredients:

- 2 slices whole-grain bread
- 1 ripe avocado, mashed
- 2 eggs (fried, poached, or scrambled)
- Salt and pepper to taste
- Red pepper flakes (optional)

Instructions:

1. Toast the bread slices to your desired level of crispiness.
2. Mash the avocado and spread it evenly on the toast.
3. Cook eggs as desired and place on top of the avocado toast.
4. Sprinkle with salt, pepper, and red pepper flakes before serving.

Garlic Parmesan Roasted Potatoes

Ingredients:

- 4 medium potatoes, cubed
- 2 tbsp olive oil
- 3 garlic cloves, minced
- 1/2 cup grated Parmesan cheese
- 1 tsp dried rosemary
- Salt and pepper to taste

Instructions:

1. Preheat oven to 400°F (200°C).
2. Toss cubed potatoes with olive oil, garlic, Parmesan, rosemary, salt, and pepper.
3. Spread the potatoes on a baking sheet and roast for 25-30 minutes, flipping halfway through, until golden and crispy.

Spicy Tuna Poke Bowl

Ingredients:

- 1/2 lb sushi-grade tuna, cubed
- 2 tbsp soy sauce
- 1 tbsp sesame oil
- 1 tsp Sriracha (adjust to taste)
- 1/2 avocado, sliced
- 1/2 cucumber, sliced
- 1/4 cup edamame
- 1 cup cooked rice (white, brown, or sushi rice)
- Sesame seeds for garnish

Instructions:

1. Mix soy sauce, sesame oil, and Sriracha in a bowl. Toss tuna in the sauce and let marinate for 10-15 minutes.
2. Assemble the bowl by layering rice, marinated tuna, avocado, cucumber, and edamame.
3. Garnish with sesame seeds and serve immediately.

Shrimp Tacos with Lime Crema

Ingredients:

- 1 lb shrimp, peeled and deveined
- 1 tbsp olive oil
- 1 tsp chili powder
- 1/2 tsp cumin
- 1/2 tsp paprika
- Salt and pepper to taste
- 8 small tortillas
- 1/2 cup sour cream
- 1 tbsp lime juice
- 1 tbsp cilantro, chopped
- 1/2 cup shredded cabbage

Instructions:

1. Toss shrimp in olive oil, chili powder, cumin, paprika, salt, and pepper.
2. Heat a pan and cook shrimp for 2-3 minutes per side until pink.
3. Mix sour cream, lime juice, and cilantro to make the crema.
4. Warm tortillas and assemble tacos with shrimp, cabbage, and a drizzle of lime crema.

Chickpea Salad Sandwich

Ingredients:

- 1 can chickpeas, drained and mashed
- 1/4 cup Greek yogurt or mayo
- 1 tbsp mustard
- 1 tbsp lemon juice
- 1/4 tsp garlic powder
- Salt and pepper to taste
- 2 slices whole grain bread
- Lettuce and tomato for garnish

Instructions:

1. In a bowl, mash chickpeas and mix with yogurt (or mayo), mustard, lemon juice, garlic powder, salt, and pepper.
2. Spread the chickpea mixture onto bread and top with lettuce and tomato.
3. Serve with a side of chips or pickles.

Beef Tacos with Salsa Verde

Ingredients:

- 1 lb ground beef
- 1 tsp cumin
- 1 tsp chili powder
- Salt and pepper to taste
- 8 small tortillas
- 1/2 cup salsa verde
- Optional toppings: shredded lettuce, cheese, sour cream, diced tomatoes

Instructions:

1. Cook ground beef in a skillet over medium heat until browned. Drain excess fat.
2. Add cumin, chili powder, salt, and pepper. Stir to combine.
3. Warm tortillas and fill with seasoned beef.
4. Drizzle with salsa verde and add desired toppings.

Chicken Parmesan

Ingredients:

- 2 boneless chicken breasts, halved and pounded thin
- 1 cup breadcrumbs
- 1/2 cup grated Parmesan cheese
- 1 egg, beaten
- 1 cup marinara sauce
- 1 cup shredded mozzarella cheese
- Olive oil for frying

Instructions:

1. Preheat oven to 375°F (190°C).
2. Mix breadcrumbs and Parmesan. Dip chicken in egg, then breadcrumb mixture.
3. Pan-fry in olive oil until golden.
4. Transfer to a baking dish, top with marinara and mozzarella.
5. Bake for 20 minutes or until cheese is melted and bubbly.

Stuffed Bell Peppers

Ingredients:

- 4 bell peppers, tops removed and seeds cleaned
- 1/2 lb ground beef or turkey
- 1 cup cooked rice
- 1/2 onion, diced
- 1 cup tomato sauce
- 1/2 cup shredded cheese
- Salt and pepper

Instructions:

1. Preheat oven to 375°F (190°C).
2. Cook ground meat with onion, season with salt and pepper.
3. Stir in cooked rice and half the tomato sauce.
4. Fill each bell pepper with mixture and top with remaining sauce.
5. Bake for 30 minutes. Sprinkle cheese on top and bake 10 more minutes.

Shrimp Scampi

Ingredients:

- 1 lb shrimp, peeled and deveined
- 3 tbsp butter
- 2 tbsp olive oil
- 4 garlic cloves, minced
- Juice of 1 lemon
- 1/4 cup white wine (or broth)
- Parsley and red pepper flakes for garnish
- 8 oz spaghetti or linguine

Instructions:

1. Cook pasta according to package instructions.
2. In a large pan, heat butter and olive oil. Add garlic and sauté for 1 minute.
3. Add shrimp, cook until pink (2–3 minutes per side).
4. Stir in lemon juice and wine, simmer 2 more minutes.
5. Toss with cooked pasta and garnish with parsley and chili flakes.

Mushroom Risotto

Ingredients:

- 1 cup Arborio rice
- 1/2 onion, finely diced
- 2 tbsp olive oil
- 1/2 cup white wine
- 4 cups warm vegetable or chicken broth
- 1 cup mushrooms, sliced
- 1/4 cup Parmesan cheese
- Salt and pepper

Instructions:

1. In a pan, sauté onion in olive oil. Add mushrooms and cook until soft.
2. Stir in rice and toast for 1–2 minutes.
3. Add wine, stir until absorbed.
4. Gradually add warm broth, 1/2 cup at a time, stirring until absorbed before adding more.
5. Once rice is creamy and tender, stir in Parmesan. Season to taste.

Tomato Basil Soup with Grilled Cheese Croutons

Ingredients:

- 1 tbsp olive oil
- 1/2 onion, chopped
- 2 garlic cloves, minced
- 1 can (28 oz) crushed tomatoes
- 1 cup vegetable broth
- 1/4 cup fresh basil, chopped
- Salt and pepper
- 2 grilled cheese sandwiches, cut into cubes

Instructions:

1. In a pot, sauté onion and garlic in olive oil until soft.
2. Add crushed tomatoes, broth, and basil. Simmer for 20 minutes.
3. Blend until smooth and season to taste.
4. Top with grilled cheese croutons before serving.

Chicken and Rice Casserole

Ingredients:

- 2 cups cooked rice
- 2 cups cooked, shredded chicken
- 1 can cream of mushroom (or chicken) soup
- 1/2 cup milk
- 1/2 cup shredded cheese
- 1/2 tsp garlic powder
- Salt and pepper

Instructions:

1. Preheat oven to 375°F (190°C).
2. In a bowl, mix all ingredients together.
3. Pour into a greased baking dish and top with extra cheese if desired.
4. Bake for 25–30 minutes until bubbly and golden on top.

Baked Chicken Fajita Bowl

Ingredients:

- 2 chicken breasts, sliced
- 1 bell pepper, sliced
- 1/2 onion, sliced
- 2 tbsp olive oil
- 1 tsp chili powder
- 1/2 tsp cumin
- Salt and pepper
- 1 cup cooked rice or quinoa

Instructions:

1. Preheat oven to 400°F (200°C).
2. Toss chicken and veggies with oil and spices.
3. Spread on a baking sheet and bake for 20–25 minutes.
4. Serve over rice or quinoa.

Roasted Vegetable Soup

Ingredients:

- 2 carrots, chopped
- 2 potatoes, chopped
- 1 zucchini, chopped
- 1 bell pepper, chopped
- 1/2 onion, chopped
- 2 tbsp olive oil
- 4 cups vegetable broth
- Salt, pepper, and thyme

Instructions:

1. Preheat oven to 400°F (200°C).
2. Toss all vegetables with olive oil, salt, and pepper. Roast for 25–30 minutes.
3. Transfer to a pot, add broth and thyme. Simmer for 15 minutes.
4. Blend partially or fully, depending on desired texture.

Avocado and Egg Breakfast Burrito

Ingredients:

- 2 large eggs
- 1/2 avocado, sliced
- 1/4 cup shredded cheese
- 1/4 cup salsa
- 1/4 cup black beans (optional)
- 1 large tortilla
- Salt and pepper to taste

Instructions:

1. Scramble eggs in a skillet over medium heat until fully cooked; season with salt and pepper.
2. Warm the tortilla and layer eggs, avocado, cheese, beans (if using), and salsa.
3. Roll into a burrito and toast in the pan for 1–2 minutes per side until golden.

Pappardelle with Creamy Mushroom Sauce

Ingredients:

- 8 oz pappardelle pasta
- 2 tbsp butter
- 2 cloves garlic, minced
- 8 oz mushrooms, sliced
- 1/2 cup heavy cream
- 1/4 cup grated Parmesan
- Salt, pepper, and parsley

Instructions:

1. Cook pappardelle according to package instructions.
2. In a skillet, melt butter and sauté garlic and mushrooms until soft.
3. Add cream, simmer until thickened, then stir in Parmesan.
4. Toss pasta in the sauce, season, and garnish with parsley.

Chicken Pot Pie

Ingredients:

- 2 cups cooked chicken, shredded
- 1 cup frozen peas and carrots
- 1/3 cup chopped onion
- 1/3 cup butter
- 1/3 cup flour
- 1 3/4 cups chicken broth
- 2/3 cup milk
- 1 pie crust

Instructions:

1. Preheat oven to 425°F (220°C).
2. In a pot, melt butter and cook onion. Stir in flour until smooth.
3. Gradually add broth and milk, cook until thickened.
4. Add chicken and veggies. Pour into a pie dish and top with crust.
5. Bake 30–35 minutes or until golden. Let sit before serving.

Spaghetti Carbonara

Ingredients:

- 8 oz spaghetti
- 2 eggs
- 1/2 cup grated Parmesan
- 4 oz pancetta or bacon, diced
- Salt and black pepper

Instructions:

1. Cook spaghetti. Reserve 1/2 cup pasta water.
2. In a skillet, cook pancetta until crisp.
3. Beat eggs with Parmesan in a bowl.
4. Quickly mix hot pasta with egg mixture, adding pasta water as needed to make a creamy sauce.
5. Add pancetta and season generously with pepper.

Roasted Garlic and Parmesan Brussels Sprouts

Ingredients:

- 1 lb Brussels sprouts, halved
- 2 tbsp olive oil
- 3 cloves garlic, minced
- 1/4 cup grated Parmesan
- Salt and pepper

Instructions:

1. Preheat oven to 400°F (200°C).
2. Toss Brussels sprouts with oil, garlic, salt, and pepper.
3. Roast for 25 minutes, then sprinkle with Parmesan and roast 5 more minutes.

Veggie and Hummus Wrap

Ingredients:

- 1 large tortilla or wrap
- 1/2 cup hummus
- 1/4 cup shredded carrots
- 1/4 cup cucumber slices
- 1/4 cup bell pepper strips
- 1/4 avocado, sliced
- A handful of spinach or greens

Instructions:

1. Spread hummus over tortilla.
2. Layer veggies and avocado.
3. Roll tightly into a wrap and slice in half.

Sloppy Joes

Ingredients:

- 1 lb ground beef
- 1/2 cup chopped onion
- 1/2 cup ketchup
- 1 tbsp mustard
- 1 tbsp brown sugar
- Salt and pepper
- 4 burger buns

Instructions:

1. Cook beef and onion in a skillet until browned.
2. Stir in ketchup, mustard, sugar, salt, and pepper. Simmer 10 minutes.
3. Serve on toasted buns.

Lemon Basil Pesto Chicken

Ingredients:

- 2 boneless chicken breasts
- 2 tbsp lemon juice
- 1/4 cup basil pesto
- Salt and pepper
- Olive oil

Instructions:

1. Preheat oven to 375°F (190°C).
2. Season chicken with salt and pepper.
3. In a pan, sear chicken for 2–3 minutes per side.
4. Place in baking dish, top with pesto and lemon juice. Bake for 20 minutes.

Sausage and Peppers

Ingredients:

- 1 lb Italian sausage (sliced or whole)
- 2 bell peppers, sliced
- 1 onion, sliced
- 2 tbsp olive oil
- 1 tsp garlic powder
- Salt and pepper

Instructions:

1. Heat oil in a large skillet over medium heat. Add sausage and brown on all sides.
2. Add peppers, onion, garlic powder, salt, and pepper.
3. Cook until veggies are tender and sausage is cooked through, about 15–20 minutes.

Grilled Veggie Skewers with Quinoa

Ingredients:

- 1 zucchini, sliced
- 1 red bell pepper, chopped
- 1 red onion, chopped
- 1 cup cherry tomatoes
- 2 tbsp olive oil
- Salt, pepper, dried oregano
- 1 cup quinoa, rinsed

Instructions:

1. Cook quinoa per package instructions.
2. Toss veggies with olive oil, salt, pepper, and oregano. Thread onto skewers.
3. Grill or roast at 425°F (220°C) for 15–20 minutes, turning once.
4. Serve skewers over quinoa.

Baked Salmon with Asparagus

Ingredients:

- 2 salmon fillets
- 1 bunch asparagus, trimmed
- 2 tbsp olive oil
- 2 cloves garlic, minced
- 1 lemon, sliced
- Salt and pepper

Instructions:

1. Preheat oven to 400°F (200°C).
2. Place salmon and asparagus on a baking sheet. Drizzle with oil, garlic, salt, and pepper.
3. Top salmon with lemon slices.
4. Bake for 15–18 minutes or until salmon flakes easily.

Stuffed Portobello Mushrooms

Ingredients:

- 4 large portobello caps
- 1 cup spinach, chopped
- 1/2 cup ricotta or goat cheese
- 1/4 cup Parmesan, grated
- 1 garlic clove, minced
- Olive oil, salt, and pepper

Instructions:

1. Preheat oven to 375°F (190°C).
2. Remove mushroom stems and brush caps with oil.
3. Mix spinach, cheese, garlic, salt, and pepper.
4. Fill mushrooms with the mixture and top with Parmesan.
5. Bake 20–25 minutes until mushrooms are tender.

Sweet Potato and Chickpea Curry

Ingredients:

- 1 tbsp oil
- 1 onion, chopped
- 2 cloves garlic, minced
- 1 tbsp curry powder
- 2 medium sweet potatoes, cubed
- 1 can chickpeas, drained
- 1 can coconut milk
- Salt and pepper

Instructions:

1. Sauté onion and garlic in oil until soft.
2. Stir in curry powder, sweet potatoes, and chickpeas.
3. Add coconut milk, bring to a simmer, cover and cook for 20 minutes or until potatoes are soft.
4. Season to taste and serve with rice or naan.

Chicken Shawarma Bowls

Ingredients:

- 2 chicken breasts, sliced
- 1 tbsp olive oil
- 1 tsp each cumin, paprika, garlic powder, and turmeric
- 1/2 tsp cinnamon
- Salt and pepper
- 1 cup cooked rice or couscous
- Toppings: diced cucumber, tomato, red onion, tahini or yogurt sauce

Instructions:

1. Toss chicken with oil and spices. Marinate for 30 minutes if possible.
2. Cook in a skillet until browned and cooked through.
3. Assemble bowls with rice, chicken, veggies, and sauce.

www.ingramcontent.com/pod-product-compliance
Lightning Source LLC
LaVergne TN
LVHW081325060526
838201LV00055B/2460